Between TICK and TOCK

What the Bible says
about how it all begins,
how it all ends,
and everything
in between.

MICHAEL P. JENSEN

a. Acorn Press

Published by Acorn Press
An imprint of Bible Society Australia
ACN 148 058 306 | Charity licence 19 000 528
GPO Box 4161
Sydney NSW 2001
Australia
www.acornpress.net.au | www.biblesociety.org.au

ISBN 978-0-647-53293-5

First published by Morning Star Publishing in 2020,
ISBN 978-0-647-53068-9

Michael P. Jensen asserts his right under section 193 of the
Copyright Act 1968 (Cth) to be identified as the author of this work.

A catalogue record for this
work is available from the
NATIONAL LIBRARY OF AUSTRALIA
National Library of Australia

Cover and text design and layout by John Healy

For the parishioners of St Mark's Darling Point, Sydney

Philippians 4:1

CONTENTS

Preface

The idea for this book came from a conversation with a friend of mine, Rev Dr Peter Sanlon. He had in mind a series of books for non-specialist readers that would show how deeply interconnected Christian doctrine is. The best way to understand, say, the cross, is to see how it affects, and in turn is affected, by the way we think about creation, our humanity, and the last things. Peter had the idea for three sections in each book: *Look,* in which you'd get an overview of what the Bible says; *Link,* in which you'd see how each doctrine meshes with all the others; and *Live.* This last section is vital, because Christian doctrine is not an abstract or irrelevant thing. It shapes how we live in profound and immediate ways.

That explains the three-part structure of this book 'Between Tick and Tock'. I've also added three Appendices, because the doctrine of creation and new creation is beset by controversial issues around the role of science, the last things, and what we may call 'the spiritual creation' – angels, demons, and so on. Avoiding these juicy topics seemed like a bad idea! I've offered my take on these three issues, but I hope that a reader won't be put off by finding something to disagree with in those pages.

Look

1. Between tick and tock

When I was growing up, our church used to hold its weekends away – which we rather quaintly called 'house parties' – in a grand, stately home to the west of Sydney.

I vividly remember that house with its many corridors and its sweeping lawns and its rose gardens and its big open fireplace with gigantic logs burning away. But I particularly remember the grandfather clock that stood in its entrance hall. The grandfather clock was a somewhat solemn presence, doing its duty hour by hour. Just as a child could spend a hour gazing into the open fire, so it was transfixing to watch the swing of its heavily weighted pendulum. The clock marked the seconds with an opening beat – a 'tick' – and a closing beat, which was its opposite – a 'tock'. And as I sat watching the slow swing of the pendulum, I couldn't help feeling that the upswing of the tick was almost like a question that asked for the downswing of the tock as its answer. The tick on its own would just hang in the air, unresolved. It almost *needed* the tock.

You get the same feeling when you come to the closing bars of a piece of music. There are patterns of chords that, when you play them, seem almost to tell us what the final chord must be. There *has* to be a resolution. We anticipate it in our minds, and a good composer will tease us a little by not giving it to us quite when we expect. But the game of music involves a beginning which points towards an end. And when we are in the middle of it, when we've heard the beginning, we are pulled inexorably towards the end that must surely come. Musicians call these resolving sequences of chords 'cadences'.

Both of these experiences grab us because they remind us about the very human experience of living in time. The clock and the piece of music both tell us that there is a beginning; and that if there is a beginning, then it points towards some ending. We live in the middle of time, in between some beginning and some ending, some start which anticipates some conclusion. And just as the upswing of the clock's tick is a prophecy of its down-swinging tock, so the idea that we've begun at some point is a pointer towards an inevitable end.

That's where we have to live. We can't really choose a different, timeless existence for ourselves – just as we can't choose to live in a place without air. Time is a part of our very being as human creatures. 'Where can we live but days?' writes the great English poet Philip Larkin; and the answer to his question is, naturally, *nowhere.* Time is our home. But time is finite, as far as we can understand it. It has brackets around it. Beginning and end.

This is a cosmic as well as a personal reality. We know that everything around us was not always that way. It must have begun somewhere, somewhen. And with that, we know that it won't last eternally, either – at least not as it is. All things must pass. The universe expands, and at some stage it will be done with expanding, and will contract, and everything we recognise will be destroyed.

This is what happens to us, too. Our parents tell us about our birthdays. They know that we did not exist from the beginning of all things because they were present at our coming into being. And with that knowledge comes the knowledge that the upswing, the tick, of birth is to be answered by the downswing, the tock, of death. Our growth into life is an anticipation of our leaving it behind, one day.

And this is our curse as human beings, because even though we are bracketed by some beginning and some end, we can imagine what it might be like for it not to be so. We have a deep longing to transcend our limits. We dream of not being defeated ultimately by time working its cruel alchemy on our bodies, but rather of living on. The miracle of our consciousness seems like it is poorly matched to our bodies. Our hunger for life does not usually abate even when our bodies shrivel.

As an Anglican parish minister, I've presided at many funerals. One of the things I notice is that even the most hardened atheist cannot finally come at the thought of the disintegration of the human personality. It is one thing to argue that there is no life after death in the pub over a few drinks. It is quite another to stand beside the coffin of a loved one and say the same. The sense that human being is made for something more than this end is so deeply rooted, so powerful, that even non-religious people feel they have to reach for something – usually some vague sense that the dead person is now 'up there'.

What we say to ourselves about the beginning and ending of all things is also a way of making sense of the middle. It's a way of finding meaning. If we can understand what the tick anticipates, and trace its direction, then we can grasp something of what the swirl of events in between might mean. Shakespeare's Macbeth, when he was at his lowest ebb, speculated that life is 'a tale told by an idiot, full of sound and fury, signifying nothing'. That was because he had become convinced that his life was heading towards a calamitous ending. He had been fooled into thinking that his destiny was rather different, and had pursued a ruinous and murderous course of action 'in the middle'. That sense of what an ending might be shapes our understanding of what we should do in the meantime. The 19 terrorists who flew into the World Trade Center in 2001 understood themselves as heading, not towards a fiery end, but through a fiery ordeal to a paradise granted to them because they had committed their act of destruction.

Human experience, that is to say, seems to shape itself into a story of some kind. Stories, as we know from a very early age, have different endings. A tragedy and a comedy end differently. They may both begin with 'once upon a time', but only one of them may end with 'and they all lived happily ever after'. And the end of the story transforms the meaning of its middle. It is no surprise to us that Hamlet dies. He's not principally an action hero, but a tragic hero. His quest to avenge his father is both necessary and doomed. If (say) Bruce Willis were to offer a version of Hamlet, it would be a very different story. It would mean something else – our understanding of the action in the middle of the play would be entirely different. We would be admirers of Hamlet's self-discipline and his courage – how does he overcome his feelings of self-doubt and the moral complexity of his situation?

What then, should we think about endings and beginnings? The problem is that, although the natural world seems to suggest to us that there *is* a connected and meaningful story, it doesn't reveal to us without ambiguity what that story might be. Staring at an extraordinary sunset has left many human beings

6

thinking there simply must be more to existence than the mechanical round of life and death. Something transcendent seems to radiate through the natural order, seems to permeate it with beauty and purpose. But … what is it? We cannot easily tell. And for every scene of beauty, where everything seems fitting and ordered, we will also be able to recall instances of banality and terror.

Christian theology starts with the premise that this intuition we have about the order and beauty and purpose of the creation is right, and that it has been confirmed by the Creator himself. He has reached over the gap separating time from eternity, and has spoken to us. What meaning is there in human life? We cannot deduce it, though we can suspect that it is there. But if it is *revealed* to us, then that's a different matter. Then we are given a starting point for understanding ourselves and our world, and a frame around which we can organise our thinking.

This book is about what God reveals to us in the Bible, and about what Christians have tried to understand, about the beginnings and the endings of all things. Our purpose is bound up in the question of why we were made by the creator in the first place, and from what. What kind of world is it that we are in? And where is it heading? Can we expect the original purpose given to all things to be reached? What might give us that confidence, since we can't see the present from the future? We will return to the Bible's response to these questions in due course. But it is worth saying from the outset that the Bible plunges us right into the world in the middle. It is a book written by and about and for people who experience life in between the tick and the tock. While it describes for the world before the tick and after the tock, it does so by stretching language as far as it will go. It does not claim to transport us to another realm of existence. Rather, its claim is always the opposite: that the eternal one, himself not subject to time, enters time and discloses himself to us.

In other words: the Bible tells us a particular *story* about the beginning and end of all things, and about our own beginning and end. Narrative (or plot, or story) will be vital categories for us to keep in mind, because the Bible does not give us a set of abstract principles or philosophical theorems. Even as we isolate propositions to consider, we must never forget that Christianity tells a story about events that it claims happened in history, and about a particular ending that it claims will come. Even the great creeds of the Christian church, which look as if they just list a set of truths, tell a great story: the story of the Creator and his creation; of the redeemer, Jesus Christ, who was born, suffered, died, rose again and ascended, and who will come to judge the world; and of the Holy Spirit, who, in the middle of time between the end the beginning, ministers to the people of God.

2. Alternative ticks and tocks

Human beings have a deep sense that there is a beginning and an end – both to all things and to themselves. And what they think these are shapes what they understand themselves to be doing in the in-between time. At the same time, there's a profound sense that human beings have always shared that they are made for something more than the limits of time. That paradox tells us a great deal about human experience.

What are some of the ways that human beings have

described the origins of all things and the future to come? What are some of the stories we tell each other?

a. Polytheism

Polytheism, as is well known, involves the worship of many gods. Many, if not most, human cultures in history have been polytheistic in their outlook. Polytheists often do say there is one god or deity who is bigger than all the rest, or older, and who may have been the originator of the others. But the myths of polytheistic religions usually see the creation of the world and of human beings as the by-product of a divine struggle.

Take the Babylonian creation myth call *Enuma Elish.* It starts with two gods, a husband and wife called Apsu and Tiamat. Apsu is the god of fresh water and Tiamat god of the oceans, who looks like a sea-serpent. Then several other gods are created, and they take up residence in Tiamat's body. But these gods make such a racket that Tiamat and Apsu become really angry. Apsu wants to have them killed, but Tiamat warns Ea, who is the most powerful god living in his body. Ea puts a spell on Apsu, and has him killed, which means that Ea is now the chief god. He marries Damkina and has a son called Marduk.

Marduk is an even greater god than those before him. And – to cut a very long story short – Marduk eventually challenges Tiamat to a battle. Victorious over her, he cuts her dead body into two, and makes the earth and the sky from the pieces. He then proceeded to create the patterns of the stars and the planets, sun and moon. From the blood of another defeated god, Kingu, mixed with clay, Marduk made human beings to do the work of the gods.

Meanwhile, in Scandinavia, they told the story somewhat like this. Odin is the oldest and most powerful of the gods, and has always ruled all things. He created heaven and earth, and human beings. But there was a time before him. When there was nothing, the frost giant Ymir came into being. Ymir was evil. Odin, who had emerged from the ice, hated Ymir and, with his brothers, killed him. The narrator takes up the gruesome tale:

> From Ymir's flesh, Odin and his brothers made the earth, and from his shattered bones and teeth, they made the rocks and stones. From Ymir's blood, they made the rivers and lakes, and they circled the earth with an ocean of blood. Ymir's skull they made into the sky, secured at four points by four dwarfs named East, West, North and South... From Ymir's brains, they shaped the clouds.

These dramatic tales, though they are very different, contain some telling similarities. For one thing, the creation emerges from a violent struggle between good and evil. It is a by-product of something else. If the earth is really the fallen body of a giant, or the slain corpse of a sea-monster, what kind of a thing is it? It has a kind of terrible, even awesome beauty, but not much more. It is not intentionally made, but accidentally happens.

And what of human beings? They inhabit a lower realm where they have to, in some way, hope that the gods do not inflict more harm on them with their hidden and heavenly politics. The best we can do is try to appease the spirits and divinities that surround us and inhabit the things around us. Most polytheistic religions practice some system of sacrifice in order to please the relevant god or goddess.

And what kind of end can we expect? If struggle between the gods began creation, then we can expect that renewed struggle will probably end it. Mostly in polytheistic religions, the individual soul carries on in a shadowy place of the dead. It may be that some great souls ascend to divinity themselves, but to become a god means becoming a participant in the divine wrangle that pits god against god. It may be, that as the dead, we will be able to have some influence over life on earth.

b. Pantheism

An equally ancient alternative to polytheism is pantheism. Now, sometimes a polytheist and pantheist may overlap in their beliefs, or live inside the same religious super-structure. Is Hinduism polytheist or pantheist, or example? The best answer is probably 'yes'!

Pantheists believe that God, or divinity, and the world are not separate. God is not distinct from the universe but rather is identical to it. God is not 'up there' but rather 'all around'. The epic *Star Wars* takes place in a basically pantheistic universe permeated by 'the force' – a mysterious divine-like being that is accessible through mystical powers of concentration to the Jedi. In *The Lion King*, too, we hear talk of 'the circle of life', a kind of divine presence that fills all living things.

For pantheists (though we have to generalise here, because pantheists are quite diverse), the being of the universe has no beginning and no end. Ordinary theists will think of God as having attributes like omnipresence and omnipotence and eternity. If you transfer these on to the universe, you start to 'get' pantheism. Pantheists see the cosmos as eternal – history is not a line from chaos to order or from order to chaos, but rather a circle. There is no particular final end point; neither was there any particular beginning. There is in fact a series of beginnings, which were endings of other beginnings,

11

themselves also endings (if you see what I mean).

Traditionally, pantheists see that the goal of human life is to become one with the universe – which means the individual has no ultimate significance. If all is god, then I am god, or at least, I share the divinity of the universe – but this is not a kind of narcissism. Quite the opposite is the case: my goal is to dissolve into the universe and become part of it. Mind you, the more westernised pantheism becomes, the more the individual returns, because we westerners just can't imagine a universe where we are not the centre.

Albert Einstein was a self-declared pantheist. For him, this meant that he did not believe in a personal God, though he was not an atheist. He declared that he did not believe in life after death. He said once: 'I believe in [a] God, who reveals himself in the harmony of all that exists, not in a God who concerns himself with the fate and the doings of mankind.'

He also wrote:

> Scientific research can reduce superstition by encouraging people to think and view things in terms of cause and effect. Certain it is that a conviction, akin to religious feeling, of the rationality and intelligibility of the world lies behind all scientific work of a higher order. [...] This firm belief, a belief bound up with a deep feeling, in a superior mind that reveals itself in the world of experience, represents my conception of God. In common parlance this may be described as 'pantheistic'.

What does human life look like in such a world? The God who is revealed in the 'harmony of all that exists' sounds on the face of it a peaceable character. But think about the 'natural' world for a moment: how harmonious is it? What does the pantheist make of what we might call 'evil'? Is it part of the 'harmony', or not? If it is, then this harmony is not very comforting, for the forces of the universe have conspired to produce an unyielding and unsympathetic experience for many human beings. As Einstein says, the deity he believes in isn't much concerned with the doings of human beings – so we are pretty much left to interact with whatever God is by observing the natural world. Which makes scientists akin to priests of course.

Furthermore, the pantheist is committed to trying to understand good and evil somehow from what exists around him or her in the universe. There is no source of intervening revelation to give guidance, but only what the human mind can reason from the ground up. And yet, this proves a very difficult thing to do, in fact – to move from what 'is', to what 'ought'. There are examples of cannibalism in the animal world, for example; but does this justify cannibalism among human beings? Few would agree that it does.

c. Naturalism

Naturalism is the view that there is only the material world and nothing else. There is no force outside the natural world that caused it to come to be; and only the physical chain of causes and effects will end all things. Theologically speaking, naturalists are atheists. Their worldview has no place for God as a designer or shaper. There is no meaning given to the order of things from outside.

The current consensus among naturalist philosophers and scientists is that the universe began some 14.5 billion years ago with the so-called 'Big Bang' – an explosion of an extremely dense point of matter. The extraordinary forces unleashed then have produced a universe so large that the extremely finely balanced conditions on Earth – which seem so unlikely to have come about by chance alone – were at least somewhat probable. A naturalist would argue that the sheer size of the universe, and the time available, mean that life on an earth-like planet had to happen sometime. It's just as if you asked me to roll five double sixes in a row on a set of dice. The probability of this happening is very low, but, given enough time – it may take a year – it will come to pass. That's why, to increase the probability of life existing, scientists now talk about other universes.

Life then emerged on planet Earth, and, piece by piece, bit by bit, evolved. There was no hand to guide this process, no divine eye watching over it or planning it out. The arrival of human beings relatively late on the scene is product of a massive winnowing process. We have been moulded and refined by the need to pass on our genes.

Now, in principle, naturalists may change their minds about all this, since they are committed to the idea that the natural world is what we have to work with, and we may discover more evidence – or be swayed by a different interpretation of the evidence. Nevertheless, the current story told by naturalists is very widely held. The 'tick' that sets everything in motion was not a personal design or decision, it was the explosion of physical forces that did not think of anything. What our minds emerged from is not other minds, but from a combination of physical forces acting on matter over billions of years. We are not, then, as beings, made for any particular purpose. We are just *here*, to make of our existence what we will, or at least, what we can given the limitations bequeathed to us by the circumstances in which we live. As Richard Dawkins writes in his best seller *The God Delusion*:

In a universe of blind physical forces and genetic replication, some people are going to get hurt, other people are going to get lucky, and you won't find any rhyme or reason in it, nor any justice. The universe we observe has precisely the properties we should expect if there is, at the bottom, no design, no purpose, no evil and no other good. Nothing but blind, pitiless indifference. DNA neither knows nor cares. DNA just is. And we dance to its music.

And the 'tock'? Well, the physical decay of the universe is already set in motion. Our sun will run out of fuel. The forces of the expanding universe will one day be spent and everything will collapse back in on itself. And that will be that. But our own personal demise is closer than that. We will die, and that will be the end of our conscious self, since there is no life after death. The span of life we have been given by the universe is simply what it is. And it is in these years that we must live, and love, and find pleasure such as we can, and do what we are called to do.

Most naturalists don't end up as nihilists. That is, most naturalists, even Richard Dawkins, find the pull of talking about the meaning and purpose of human life too strong to resist. They will talk about human rights, and about the mission of human beings, and so on. Full bore nihilism is a very hard creed to like. Mostly, we hunger for purpose and meaning, so we might as well invent a purpose while we are here, before the grim *tock* of death brings down the shutters on our small glimpse of conscious life. Marxists, for example, don't believe in God, but do imagine that history has a particular trajectory, pulling us towards a Marxist utopia, in which there is finally no private property. Existentialists urge human beings to make their own individual meaning out of their circumstances.

Hedonists simply say we should 'look on the bright side of life' and just enjoy the ride while it lasts. All of these versions of naturalism fight against the inevitability of the hard landing that is death.

3. The Christian story

We've explored three alternative ways to think about the tick and tock of human existence. How we think things began, and how we imagine that they'll end, shape what we think we are doing in the middle of time. Are we living in a world that is planned, and if so, what is the plan and who is the planner?

It almost goes without saying that the Christian Bible has a distinct sense of time and its meaning. Christians live with a sense that they are created, and that the creator is a personal God who has destined the cosmos for his glory. The tick that the Bible describes is a distinct point of beginning, full of intent and purpose. The creator God sets all things in train, and then shapes them to their final purpose. We cannot, in Christian thinking, work this out simply by studying the world itself. We can get a sense from the world that there is an eternal destiny and a divine person, but not much more (Rom 1:18). In order to understand the shape of the story, we need the story told to us by the one who knows it. It needs to be revealed to us. That is why we turn to the pages of the Bible to understand what God says about himself and the world.

But before we do that, I want to pause a little to reflect about how we do this. One of the controversies that has dogged the Christian church in the last century and a half is the difficulty of squaring the accounts of Genesis with what modern scientific consensus is claiming about the origins of the world and of human life. I'll say a little bit more about that in Appendix A. This controversy has had the effect of placing undue emphasis on the opening chapters of Genesis for our understanding of the beginning of all things. What we should not fail to notice is that there are other passages of the Bible – in particular Psalm 104, Job 28, and Proverbs 8 – that paint their own pictures of the creation. We also need to read these Old Testament texts, as Christians are always called upon to do, from the perspective of the New Testament. What we are trying to do in reading Scripture is to understand it as a whole. We need to synthesise these accounts rather than neglect some in favour of one.

Here, then, is an outline of a Christian theology of the tick and the tock.

a. God is not the world

The first principle of a Christian view of the world is that God is not it, and it is not God. When Genesis 1:1 kicks off the Bible by saying 'In the beginning' – words which are echoed by John in the beginning of his gospel – it is saying that there was a time before the creation existed. The creation begins. God does not begin. He is not made. He simply *is*. And though he creates the world, he does not create it as an extension of his being. It is different in nature to him. He has a divine nature; the cosmos, while it shows his imprint and reveals his character, does not have a divine nature.

An easy way to see this is to note how Israel was called upon to worship the one God, the Lord, exclusively and uniquely. The world was not subject to the competitions of many gods for supremacy. And neither was it permissible to worship idols, which are themselves parts of the created order. This point is made very sharply by the prophet Isaiah. He describes a carpenter cutting down a tree:

> Half of the wood he burns in the fire;
>   over it he prepares his meal,
>   he roasts his meat and eats his fill.
> He also warms himself and says,
>   'Ah! I am warm; I see the fire.'
> From the rest he makes a god, his idol;
>   he bows down to it and worships.
> He prays to it and says,
>   'Save me! You are my god!' (Is 44:16-17)

You could never worship the God of Israel this way, because he does not inhabit material objects in this way. He is fundamentally different from the creation. He is invisible. He is spirit.

As a side note, it's interesting to note how often objections to the existence of God imagine him as an object in the physical universe. This is the problem with the 'who made God?' objection. This would be a problem if God were like any other object in the material world. But the biblical understanding of God is not of him as a part of the material universe. He *enters* it, and engages with it, for sure. But he is not constrained by the laws of physics since he is not part of the realm that is governed by these laws. Who made God? No-one. He is eternal.

b. He creates by his word

How does God create the world? Some parts of the Bible talk poetically about the way he moulds things, as if he took pre-existing material and shaped it:

> The sea is his, for he made it,
>   and his hands formed the dry land. (Ps 95:5).

Other passages use words like 'create' and 'make', which don't tell us much about how God created the world.

But Genesis 1 gives a vivid description of the means by which God created all things. It comes in the formula 'And God said...and it was so' which is used throughout the passage. The creator creates by speaking. His fundamental activity in creating the universe is talking. He says it, and it is.

This tells us a great deal. In the first place, the creation is not formed as an accidental by-product of a primeval struggle between the gods. The creation is not the fallen corpse of a sea-monster or a giant. It is no by-product. It is the intentional creation of a supreme being who is in full control of his actions. It is created without struggle. This means that the creator is supremely powerful to order and to purpose his creation. It has a plan and a purpose that come from its creator. It is designed by a designer, carefully and beautifully.

In Proverbs 8, the writer uses the device of personifying God's wisdom as his companion in the creation:

I was there when he set the heavens in place,
  when he marked out the horizon on the face of the deep,
when he established the clouds above
  and fixed securely the fountains of the deep,
when he gave the sea its boundary
  so that the waters would not overstep his command,
and when he marked out the foundations of the earth.
(Prov 8:27-29)

That's another way of saying that God created the world by his word. It is a product of his wisdom. It comes from his genius and from no-one else.

We'll return to this theme in chapter 2, because it is incredibly significant that Jesus is called 'the Word of God' in the New Testament.

c. He creates from nothing

Christianity has always insisted that God created all things from nothing, or *ex nihilo.* Even though this is not, strictly speaking, the picture that we have in Genesis 1 or in Genesis 2, Christians have always thought that God's sheer independence of the creation he makes and its utter dependence on him means that he doesn't create from pre-existent raw material. That would mean that there is some other thing that is eternal other than God, or some other creator. Eternity belongs to God alone.

Scripture repeatedly insists that God created 'all things' – which, we can assume, means the things from which he created other things. He forms us from the dust of the ground, which he has in turn made. In Romans 4:17 we read that God is 'the God who gives life to the dead and calls into being things that were not'. The parallel with the resurrection is instructive. God makes to exist those things which once had no existence. Without him they do not have existence. He makes them, that is to say, from nothing.

d. He calls it 'good'

One of the features of the text of Genesis 1 is the repetition of the word 'good'. God calls his creation 'good', and ultimately 'very good'. His work is pleasing to him. It is not, a place that he disdained. Even though it is not divine and does not have a divine nature, it is the good work of a good God who calls it 'good'. Good in what sense? It is ordered, productive, delightful, and full of potential. It is an expression of his divine character, and so must be good.

That creation is fundamentally 'good' is not something that

other worldviews countenance. The universe is either neutral, or the site of a mixing of good and evil, or completely evil. Only in the biblical mind is the material creation held in such high regard. The entry of evil into the world is not a permanent state but a corruption of a cosmos that was intended for high honour in the eyes of the one who made it. As the eighteenth century poet Joseph Addison wrote:

> The Spacious Firmament on high,
> With all the blue Ethereal Sky,
> And spangled Heav'ns, a Shining Frame,
> Their great Original proclaim:
> Th' unwearied Sun, from day to day,
> Does his Creator's Pow'r display,
> And publishes to every Land
> The Work of an Almighty Hand.

e. He orders it

When the creator creates, he brings his order to the creation. In Genesis 1, he separates light from dark, water from dry land, sun from moon and stars. He makes the creatures of the planet 'according to their kind'. The patterns observable in nature are there because he arranges it to be so. He makes not simply the things but the relationships between the things. Things are arranged in concert so that the goodness of the creation is not simply in the individual items in it, but in the whole of it. Our eyes are drawn to tigers and mountains, and less to deserts and rats; but the glory of the creation belongs to all of it together. Tigers and mountains aren't what they are except that there is a world with deserts and rats.

The order that God brings to the creation is of two kinds. He puts together things that belong together, 'according to its kind'. But he also brings purpose to the universe. It is ordered not only to function together, but to a particular goal that he has in mind. It is going somewhere, in other words. We get a glimpse of this in the creation of humankind, who are given the mission of filling the earth and cultivating it. The world is not yet what it could be; it is created with potential. And in the New Testament, we are told that Jesus Christ is himself the goal to which the world is heading (see for example Col 1:15-23). But more of that in chapter 2.

f. He governs it

God is not simply the creator who creates and then stands back and watches what he has caused unwind. In biblical thinking, he is thoroughly involved with the creation at every point. The intimacy of God's involvement in his creation is the theme of Psalm 139:

> For you created my inmost being;
>   you knit me together in my mother's womb.
> I praise you because I am fearfully and wonderfully made;
>   your works are wonderful,
>   I know that full well.

In theological terms, God is not simply omniscient but omnipresent. But he is present not simply as a lingering, ghostly presence, observing but helpless. He is continuing to work his purposes out in the world, governing it in every respect. The natural forces of the seasons are his doing. He makes it to rain, or to stop raining. He watches over the sparrow, and the lilies of the field, and provides for them.

What are we to make, in the first place, of the independent actions of human beings and other creatures, who seem to act without being controlled by God, and certainly not always in alignment with God's rule? This is a complex and important question which takes a good deal of unravelling. Suffice it to say that the Bible seems unembarrassed by it. It talks of human actors and God's sovereign government of the creation as parallel and compatible realities. The bottom line is that God's sovereignty *includes* and *is not defeated* by the actions of human beings. The cross is the perfect picture of this: those who killed Jesus planned a great evil, but in this evil God produced the most exquisite good of all.

Secondly, what are we to make of the presence of evil, since evil is that which God does not wish, by definition? The Christian doctrine of creation tells us that evil is an intruder into the good world that God made. It is not an eternal part of it. Neither is the experience of evil in the world the way the world is supposed to be. This gives us something very powerful to say about evil. But it is incomplete without pointing to what God intends to do *about* evil. Why does he permit that which is anathema to him? We do not ultimately know. But we do know that the end of all things that is planned by God for his good world involves the exclusion and the resolution of all that is evil. Evil's grip upon the world is only for a time.

g. It belongs to him

God governs the creation, but he does so as its owner. He has rights over it as its maker. As the creatures around the throne in Revelation 4 sing:

> 'You are worthy, our Lord and God,
>   to receive glory and honour and power,
> for you created all things,
>   and by your will they were created
>   and have their being.' (Rev 4:11)

He has deserved, in his creating of all things, the praise and honour of his creatures. In Psalm 50, God is even more explicit about ownership:

> I have no need of a bull from your stall
>   or of goats from your pens,
> for every animal of the forest is mine,
>   and the cattle on a thousand hills.
> I know every bird in the mountains,
>   and the insects in the fields are mine. (Ps 50:10-11)

It is not as if we could give him anything that isn't already his, in other words. We have everything from his hand. It belongs to him.

h. He shares it

But the Lord God is a generous God, who makes the creation in order to share it with his creatures. He invites human beings, who he makes in his image, to share in his rule of the universe. They are given capacities that resemble his: creativity, rule, ordering, rationality, wisdom. They are made of the ground, but they share his breath. He is unstintingly generous in his creation, providing its bounty for the sustenance of his creatures and for their delight. He is determined, throughout the Bible, to share his very life with creatures of flesh and blood. He is a deeply relational God, a God whose love is his hallmark. This quite persistent desire of God to share his world pushes forward the whole story of the Bible. How will his creatures respond? What will God do with their response?

i. He rests in it

The Genesis account finishes with the Lord doing something quite unexpected. Or rather, *not* doing. He rests from all the work:

> Thus the heavens and the earth were completed in all their vast array.
>
> By the seventh day God had finished the work he had been doing; so on the seventh day he rested from all his work. Then God blessed the seventh day and made it holy, because on it he rested from all the work of creating that he had done. (Gen 2:1-3)

His resting in it then becomes part of the way he commands his creatures to live in his world:

> Remember the Sabbath day by keeping it holy. Six days you shall labour and do all your work, but the seventh day is a sabbath to the Lord your God. On it you shall not do any work, neither you, nor your son or daughter, nor your male or female servant, nor your animals, nor any foreigner residing in your towns. For in six days the Lord made the heavens and the earth, the sea, and all that is in them, but he rested on the seventh day. Therefore the Lord blessed the Sabbath day and made it holy. (Ex 20:8-11)

The work-life balance of the creator is the pattern for his creatures. This is a gift to human beings (and their animals too!), for them to relish the creation and to remember the creator. As God delights in the creation they are to take delight in the creation and in him.

But the Sabbath day is also an indication that the creation is heading somewhere. It is propelled into history, a history that is complicated by the rebellion of man and woman. The Sabbath stands then not only as a reminder of the creation but of the redemption that God has in store for it. As a temporary halt to the work of God's people in the world it stands as a promise of a time when that work will cease, for God's people will be redeemed and God's creation will be restored. This is picked up of course by the author of Hebrews. The Sabbath rest not only looks backwards to God's past acts; it looks forward.

j. He cleanses it

So far we've outlined a Christian doctrine of creation mostly from the point of view of Eden before the fall.

This is really important to do, because a Christian doctrine of creation names the creation as fundamentally and originally good. The Bible plunges us into the middle of a very different experience of the world, of course. It's the world pock-marked by evil, suffering, and death. It's the world of cursed work, and fractious relationships. It's the world of Cain and Abel, not the world of Adam and Eve. We could be forgiven for thinking that it was ever thus, and that evil is as permanent as good in the world. But what we see around us is not permanent and eternal. Evil is *contingent,* which means that it is not necessary. The Bible is not fatalistic in that way.

Which means that the good God, observing the brokenness of the cosmos and the devastation wreaked by human rebellion upon it, has determined one day to bring justice, healing and reconciliation to the world. It will not last, this current state of affairs. It cannot, or God is not God. The character of God and the nature of the world he made are in and of themselves a promise that the world as we now experience it will not continue. He is holy, and his holiness means that one day he will cleanse his creation and bring his holiness to it.

We should not be in any confusion here, though. God's cleansing of his creation means that he shuts out and commits to eternal destruction all that is opposed to him and his rule.

Justice and peace depend on the exclusion of everything that stands against those things. If God's peace is to reign upon the earth it will be because those things which disrupt it are definitely and finally excluded from it. In the great vision of the renewed creation in Revelation 21, we hear God declaring:

> It is done. I am the Alpha and the Omega, the Beginning and the End. To the thirsty I will give water without cost from the spring of the water of life. Those who are victorious will inherit all this, and I will be their God and they will be my children. But the cowardly, the unbelieving, the vile, the murderers, the sexually immoral, those who practice magic arts, the idolaters and all liars—they will be consigned to the fiery lake of burning sulfur. This is the second death. (Rev 21:6-8)

Knowing this, we should read the dissonance of the present world as a sign of the glorious future that God has in store for it. One of the great passages of the New Testament brings out this theme:

> I consider that our present sufferings are not worth comparing with the glory that will be revealed in us. For the creation waits in eager expectation for the children of God to be revealed. For the creation was subjected to frustration, not by its own choice, but by the will of the one who subjected it, in hope that the creation itself will be liberated from its bondage to decay and brought into the freedom and glory of the children of God. (Rom 8:18-21)

The creation's 'bondage to decay', its frustration, is not forever. Paul writes that God has subjected the creation to this experience of limitation and entropy so that, in time, and in the way he plans it, it will be liberated along with glorious freedom of those he has saved. The Christian's experience of suffering is, therefore, a fleeting thing. It is evil and sin that pass away like the breeze. The holiness of God stands eternal and glorious, and will one day visibly fill the earth he made, so that all will know it: 'For the earth will be filled with the knowledge of the glory of the LORD as the waters cover the sea.' (Hab 2:14). In this verse there's an interesting distinction between what *is* (the glory and holiness of God fill the earth) and what is now recognised by all humankind. What is looked for here is the day when the *knowledge* of the Lord's glory fills the earth does – that is, when not only is it true, but it is recognised to be true by his creatures.

k. He renews it

The creation as we now experience it is 'old'. It is good, but distorted. It runs along with the unmistakable vestiges of its good purpose, but continually is diverted from that purpose. It will not evolve to some higher stage. History is not 'progressing', such that human beings and the world will achieve some harmonious 'sweet spot' somewhere in the future, where we can know both a just society and a good relationship with the natural world. The world needs God's cleansing, but it also needs his remaking.

The New Testament speaks of a 'new heaven and a new earth, for the old heaven and the old earth had passed away' (Rev 21:1-5). This making new of the creation will take God's creative power to accomplish. Human beings are called to prepare for it – to pray for his kingdom to come, and to live obediently under his rule. But we cannot do it. It is God's work to do. We hear in the Bible about 'the Day of the Lord' – the day of God's judgement. This will not simply be the day when human beings sit before the judgement seat of God, but the day when the whole creation itself is brought to its completion.

When will this be? Repeatedly, the New Testament says: *we don't know.* Anyone who predicts the end is therefore a charlatan to be avoided. Here's the apostle Peter's second letter: 'But the day of the Lord will come like a thief. The heavens will disappear with a roar; the elements will be destroyed by fire, and the earth and everything done in it will be laid bare.' (2 Pet 3:10)

The old earth is destined for a radical and destructive end. That much is promised, and that much we are to prepare for.

But this coming calamity is not all there is. The creation is stripped bare so that it can be renewed and remade. There is a radical discontinuity between the old creation and the new; but there is also a deep continuity. It is to 'die', but it will also be resurrected.

In fact, the resurrection of Jesus Christ from the dead is the best template we have for the coming renewal of the world. Jesus was not simply revived from the dead. He was not a zombie. His resurrection was not the same as Lazarus's – who presumably died again at a later date. When Jesus was resurrected from the dead, he was recognisable as the same person, but was also markedly different. His body, which had its wounds on it from the old creation, was glorious with a heavenly glory that is the unmistakable characteristic of the new creation.

That's an overview of the 'tick' and the 'tock', as the Bible sees it. The story of the creation, and its creator, has a distinct beginning. It was made for a good purpose by a good and powerful creator. The presence of evil in our world is a temporary diversion from that design, but not one that will stop God completing his project. In the end, there will be a new heavens and new earth, which will gleam with God's radiant glory.

Of course, I've left some crucial aspects of this story out. In fact, this way of telling the story of creation tends to obscure the one thing that makes Christian theology *Christian*: Jesus Christ. If we are to really know what the Christian version of the creation story is, then we need to start over, with Jesus Christ. In the next part of this book, I show how the Christian understanding of beginnings and endings is deeply connected with the other parts of Christian thought – and especially, that Jesus is right at the heart of a Christian account of the tick and tock.

Link

1. Israel's hope and the creation

I've promised to show how Jesus is at the centre of a Christian telling of the story of all things. But that account needs to begin with the Old Testament, which gives us the framework for understanding what Jesus was about and who he was.

The Old Testament is the story of the creator God's plan to redeem the world by his chosen people Israel. The first 11 chapters of Genesis show how human society in the good creation started to fall apart. Indeed, the world was in such turmoil and rebellion, that God decided to destroy it by water. Only one man, and his family remained to carry on the plans and promises of God: Noah. But things didn't improve.

In Genesis 12, God calls Abram somewhat out of the blue. We get no preparation for this event – nor do we have any description of how Abram (who later became Abraham) heard God's voice. What we do know is that God promised to bless this man, and through him to bless the nations of the earth.

This was the story that the people of Israel told themselves as they left Egypt under Moses' leadership and made for the Promised Land in Canaan, the land that Abraham had inhabited before them. They were the chosen people of God to be a light to the nations. Their God was not just any tribal deity with a small sphere of responsibility. He was the creator of heaven and earth himself, the Lord. His plans for them were not simply local. They were about the redemption and restoration of the whole creation itself.

This hope was thrown into radical question by the failure of Israel to be true to the God who had saved them. Their disobedience and disbelief led to catastrophe – they were exiled from their own land, and the temple was destroyed. But what then of the promises of the Almighty God? What would become of them? How could he be true to his own words, since the people he had planned to incorporate in his plans were now slaves, and their city was in ruins?

The prophets painted a vision of a day when God would provide an answer to these questions. Israel would be returned home. Their city and the temple would be rebuilt. But, most importantly, forgiveness, reconciliation, and peace would be theirs. God would once again be their God and they would be his people. He would *dwell* with them – it's a strong word of sharing mutual life. It's not too far-fetched to describe it as a marriage union. But again, this hope was not just a local hope. It had a cosmic scope. The prophet Isaiah can't help but link the renewal of the whole heavens and earth with the return and restoration of Israel:

> You heavens above, rain down my righteousness;
>   let the clouds shower it down.
> Let the earth open wide,
>   let salvation spring up,
> let righteousness flourish with it;
>   I, the Lord, have created it. (Is 45:8)

If Israel is restored, that means that the creation will have achieved its purpose. It's no mere national revival: the hope of Israel goes far deeper than that, because her God is no mere tribal deity but the maker of heaven and earth.

And that means that the coming of the Messiah, or 'Christ', the anointed Son of God, the royal prince of the house of David, destined to sit on the throne of Israel in Jerusalem, is not merely a moment in a nation's history. It is to be a moment of global, indeed *cosmic* significance. Something more than ordinary history will be happening when he comes…

2. Jesus Christ, creation, and incarnation

The coming of Jesus Christ is heralded not simply by Israel but by those outside Israel. It is signalled by the cosmos itself, for there is a sign in the stars of heaven that the King has come.

As the story of Jesus unfolds, it becomes clear that not only is his work of global scope, but that he is the presence of God with human beings to save. In Christ, the transcendent and holy God becomes a part of the creation and its history. The eternal one subjects himself to time. The one who is invisible spirit, becomes visible body. This shows us that, despite all the evil that has marred it, the creation is not utterly repellent to God. Far from it: he is committed to what he has made. It was made good, for good. God the creator still determines that this will be so, and he inhabits the physical matter of the creation to make it so. This is very different to those worldviews which would see the physical stuff of creation as weighed down, irredeemably, with evil. We do not need to escape the physical world to find God; God becomes a part of the physical world, in Christ, and finds us.

3. Jesus Christ, creation, and atonement

That God become a human being is an astonishing claim. It is interesting how difficult this has been to accept by the religious and the non-religious alike. Islam, for example, cannot imagine how the purity of God could not be sullied by contact with human flesh. On the other side, the humanist thinks of God becoming human as impossible and unnecessary.

But the incarnation of the Son of God was not, by itself, what achieved the reconciliation of all things and the restoration of the creation to its creator. Jesus Christ united God and the world in his person; but it was within this person that he offered an atoning sacrifice for the sins of human beings. Easter is the point of Christmas, if you like.

During the course of his ministry, Jesus demonstrated not just his mastery of the Scriptures and his authority to forgive sins, but also his Lordship over the creation, for example, when he stills the storm (Matt 8:23-7). It is not incidental to his ministry – it is essential that he acts within and towards the created world. When Jesus performs his miracles and heals the sick, he is showing us what the rule of God over the cosmos looks like. Even as he walked about Galilee, he was fulfilling the work of the creation.

An absolutely crucial passage for us here is Colossians 1:19-20:

> For God was pleased to have all his fullness dwell in him, and through him to reconcile to himself all things, whether things on earth or things in heaven, by making peace through his blood, shed on the cross.

Most commentators see this as part of an early hymn of the Christian church that Paul uses in his letter (as if I starting quoting 'Amazing Grace' here). And that makes it a very precious piece of writing indeed, if we imagine the first Christians singing these words to one another. We'll come back to the verses that start this hymn a bit further on, but for now we need to notice the sheer *scope* of Christ's work.

It is not simply that Jesus Christ comes to rescue a small and scattered group and take them away from the planet. Not at all. God in all his 'fullness' – his completeness – was acting in and present through Jesus Christ, in his world, with the purpose of saving and redeeming the world. And when Christ died, for the sins of the world's human actors, he made peace – a peace that extends to all things in heaven and earth. 'All things' – not just human beings, but *things* – are brought back into right relationship with their creator.

This reminds us that the impact of human rebellion against God committed the creation itself to becoming less than its glorious self. Because of Adam and Eve, the ground itself was cursed. It became, as Paul says in Romans 8, 'subjected to futility'. A pattern of decay and decline was written into the software of the cosmos.

But the death of Christ, which reconciles human beings to God by paying the penalty for human sin, likewise has a cosmic effect. Reconciliation is achieved for the stars and the atoms – though now, for a while, this process is incomplete. The non-human creation did not of course sin; but the impact of human sin was written into it. When atonement was made for human sin by Christ on the cross, the cosmos itself could wait with eager expectation for its cleansing, its completion, and its renewal.

The book of Revelation paints a picture of the destiny of all things. Praise is given not just to God as the creator of all things, but also to the slain Lamb who led his people out of captivity by his blood. All creation recognises it:

> Then I heard every creature in heaven and on earth and
> under the earth and on the sea, and all that is in them,
> saying:
> 'To him who sits on the throne and to the Lamb
>   be praise and honour and glory and power,
> for ever and ever! (Rev 5:13)

4. Jesus Christ, creation, and resurrection

Not only does Christ offer himself to the creator as a sacrifice
on behalf of the creation, he also conquers death and all that
mars and scars the world. The future of the creation is, through
Jesus Christ, a resurrected future. Several New Testament
passages link God's act of creation with the resurrection. As
we've seen, Romans 4:17 makes a parallel of them: '...the
God...who gives life to the dead and calls into existence the
things that do not exist'.

It is not surprising that we should see this link made,
because the resurrection is a demonstration of God's absolute
sovereignty over creation and his appointment of Jesus as its
ruler. The testimony of the apostles in Acts is to the lordship
of the resurrected Christ (Acts 2:32-36; 17:30-31). The
resurrection is the key to Paul's vision of the end of all things
in 1 Corinthians 15:20-28. It is also the reversal of the entry of
death into the world through Adam. The resurrection of Jesus
provides, in his body, a preview of the resurrected and renewed
creation – still corporeal, but gloriously so. The destruction
of the old creation will not spell the end of material things.
Rather, all things will be made new. As the one seated on the
throne in Revelation 21:5 says: 'Behold I make all things new!'

The resurrection also shows us how the Holy Spirit shares
in the work of the Father and the Son. He is the 'breath of life',

and it is by God's Spirit that Jesus was raised with power (Rom 1:1-5). As in creation, the Spirit brings the work of God to its fulfilment, drawing created beings like us into relationship with the Father (Rom 8:12-15). And through the Spirit, the resurrected power of the risen Lord Jesus becomes a reality in the hearts of those who believe (2 Cor 1:22).

5. Jesus Christ, the creator

The New Testament makes some extraordinary claims about Jesus of Nazareth, not the least of which is that, as the Son of God, he pre-existed the creation and was involved in the creating of the world itself. Creation was 'through Christ' (Jn 1:3, Col 1:16). What can this mean? It means that the work of the Son as Christ is not just the reason for, but the means of creating the world. In the great passages that speak of the 'cosmic' Christ, such as John1:1-3, Colossians 1:15-20 and Ephesians 1:8b-12, we find that Christ is involved in the creation 'in the beginning'; that 'in him all things hold together'; and that God will 'as a plan for the fullness of time, ... gather up all things in him, things in heaven and things on earth'. He is truly 'the first and the last' (Rev 1:17).

It's worth looking at the first verses of the Colossian hymn:

The Son is the image of the invisible God, the firstborn over all creation. For in him all things were created: things in heaven and on earth, visible and invisible, whether thrones or powers or rulers or authorities; all things have been created through him and for him. He is before all things, and in him all things hold together. And he is the head of the body, the church; he is the beginning and the firstborn from among the dead, so that in everything he might have the supremacy. (Col 1:15-18)

Just as he reconciles all things to himself in Christ, so God creates all things in Christ. They are created not just by him, but indeed for him – with him in mind. Jesus of Nazareth, then, the carpenter from Nazareth, existed before the creation of the world as the Son of God. And it was not just that he was there. It was that he shared in the making of the world. And the world was made to be the scene of his triumph and the throne of his power. What we hear of in the gospel story is not peripheral to world history. It is the heartbeat of the universe itself. The vast heavens in all their array, the mighty seas, and the electrons whirling around in every atom – all these things find their fulfilment and purpose in Jesus Christ, the Word of God.

We should note too that the 'image' language, which appeared in Genesis 1:26-28, is now used to described Jesus Christ. Jesus 'images' God, just as the first human beings should have. He fulfils the human mission to be God's emissary to his creation and to do God's work in the world.

6. The Trinity and the creation

Focusing on the role of Jesus Christ in creation and redemption leads us back to the question of the nature of God. We already have seen that Christian theology tells of a God who is the creator, who is good, who is apart from his world, and who is dedicated to it. He is Spirit, and is present in the creation that he sustains with his powerful word. His attributes are often something that distinguishes him from the material world.

Thinking of Jesus Christ, though, adds something else to our understanding of the divine nature. It is 'triune'. God was in Christ, dwelling in him in all his fullness. And Christ was with God in the beginning, and indeed *was* God (Jn 1:1-3). So what kind of divine being is this?

The answer that reflection on the Scriptures has produced is that God the creator is one God in three divine persons – Father, Son, and Holy Spirit. The creation is a work that belongs to these three persons, whose being is itself ultimate reality. In the Trinity we see unity and plurality held in perfect tension. There is one, and there are also three – a unity of different persons. In the triune being we see how God is both separate from his creation and yet intimate with it. Pantheism allows no such independence, polytheism no such connection. When we talk about the Trinity, we are speaking about the compassionate and powerful Father who rules over the creation through his incarnate Word and by his Spirit.

The world itself echoes the being of the one who made it. We have to be careful here – there are obvious dissimilarities between what is made and the one who is not, of course. But like the creator, the world is a world of relationships. There are individual entities who are what they are because of their relationship to other things in the world. There is an order to the world that is not just the individuality of things, but the distinct particularity of things in relation to other things. Things are made by God 'according to their kind', and arranged in place by him.

The other vital implication of the doctrine of the Trinity for the creation is that in it we discover that God who is one in three *loves* the world. God is love. The relationships of the Trinitarian persons are relationships of love. This love is not simply the love that binds them. It's a love that drives them beyond a kind of inward fixation. It is from this love that the creation comes to pass (Heb 1:1-14). And from this love 'for the world', the Son is given as a sacrifice for its rescue (Jn 3:16).

It would be hard to overstate the importance and distinctness of the triune God's love for the world. We understand love to be something that cannot be simply deterministic or necessary. To be love, love must be the expression of a person who is free. Love is deeply personal, in that sense. God out of his great love freely chooses to love the world – not because it is simply his job, but because of who he is and chooses to be. The Son, for love of the world, goes freely to the cross and offers his blood for its sake. If he had not freely chosen to do this, it would be not an act of sacrifice but simply a murder. However, God's love for the things he has made means that the Son empties himself of everything that he has by right, and pursues the extraordinary path of humility in obedience, to the point of death on cross.

7. The image renewed

What does all this mean for our humanity? The focus of this book is on the creation as a whole and not on the human part of it. But you can't talk about creation without talking about human beings. In the first place, this is because it is human beings who are the pinnacle of God's creative activity in Genesis 1, the only creatures who are made 'in the image and likeness of God' himself. Only human beings are commissioned to be God's agents in the world, and given dominion over the other creatures. Secondly, the responsibility for the captivity of the creation to sin and evil lies with human beings, uniquely. Thirdly, it is with a human being, made in the image of the invisible God, that we see the defeat of evil and the forgiveness of sin achieved.

With all this, we have a unique insight into the purpose of our creation and our re-creation. Human beings are made for the loving service of the world in which God has put them. They were to tune it to the praise of its creator – to order it, to fill it, to cultivate it, to make it productive, and more beautiful. We are to do things that God would have done on the earth – to reflect his holy character in every corner of the planet. We are not to destroy or exploit it, but rather lovingly to tend it. This perspective shows us how terrible the ecological crisis is, because it is not only destruction of the environment but a corruption of our own original purpose. We were not made to rape and destroy the earth, but to lovingly tend it.

What of human life now that Christ, the true image of God and the exact imprint of his being in human form, has come? The Christian knows a second life, a being born 'from above' (Jn 3:3). She has the Holy Spirit, the Spirit by which the world was created, and the same Spirit which animated living things in the first place. This new form of human life is redirected to its original purpose. Two of Paul's comments show this. In Romans 8:29, he writes: 'For those God foreknew he also predestined to be conformed to the image of his Son…' In 2 Corinthians 3:18 he writes: 'And we all… are being transformed into his image with ever-increasing glory, which comes from the Lord, who is the Spirit.'

For Christians, the work of the Holy Spirit is to make us more like Christ, who is the true image of God, just as human beings were originally made to be. When we imitate Christ, we discover our true humanity. And what was that? We fulfil more completely our servant leadership over the creation. We discover more richly our calling to sacrificial love of one another. And we worship the Lord of creation with our actions and with our words. In us, the Creator is glorified. As we become more Christ-like, then, we become more truly what we were made to be.

But also, it means that the Christian life is not a process of escaping from our bodies to become more 'spiritual'. To be more spiritual is precisely to live in our bodies, in the material world, as we wait for their 'liberation' (as Paul puts it in Romans 8). While we know that this world awaits renewal and re-creation, we do not despise it or withdraw from it. The spiritual and the physical are not, as Christians see it, opposites.

8. Jesus Christ, creation, and revelation

Lastly, we come to the doctrine that is often the starting point of Christian theology: the doctrine of revelation. How does God make himself known? What does he tell us about himself and by what means?

In a way the answer is the sum of all that has gone before. It's fascinating that God creates by his Word; and that in John 1, that Word turns out to be the Son of God. The word 'Word' is obviously a word of communication. In creating then, God communicates himself. He shows himself to and in the universe he makes. The deep order of the world is knit together as an expression of his very nature. His signature is on everything that he has made – if we have eyes to see it.

And that's the vital point, for although God's divine nature should be seen in the creation, and though on that account alone men and women should worship him, that is not what happens, as we know. We find him obscure, or only ambiguously revealed in what is. The problem is one of our distorted perception. He is certainly telling us of himself in the cosmos, but we are, in general, not good at seeing it. We are not attuned to him, even though the world is the perfect amplifier of the glory of God.

This means that it is not unimportant that we see that the world is an ordered and meaningful place – even when our experience tells us otherwise. The world is constructed as a place in which God may speak to his creatures. The invisible God is right at home communicating in the world he made. We human beings experience successful communication in this world regularly. We speak using our developed instruments of language and our other tools and we get through to one another, mostly. It is not surprising that God is capable of communicating with this world that he is made.

And God is not finished revealing himself with simply speaking the world into existence. The world and its history are shaped to speak forth the name of Jesus Christ, so that we might know once more of the God who made all things. We can understand him when he speaks, because he expresses himself in meaningful human language. In fact, he takes on human flesh to make himself known: 'No-one has ever seen God… but God the one and only Son… has made him known. '(Jn 1:18)

The great reformer John Calvin used to say that God 'lisps' to us, like a nursemaid talking in baby-talk to a child. That is, God frames himself into the world he made to speak to us, so that our limited human minds can hear him and know him. He comes to us on our terms, within the world that he made. And speaks, not in some unintelligible alien language that is beyond us, but in human words.

Live

1. What's the time?

If this is the true story of the world, how should we then live? If we human beings inhabit a world which was created by a loving, powerful, and purposeful God, but which is broken by our rebellion against that God, who yet still loves the world enough to redeem it, and will one day remake the cosmos, cleansing it from all evil and filling it with his glory, then: what now? What does life look like between the 'tick' of creation and the 'tock' of the re-creation? Jesus told his disciples the parable of the unready bridesmaids, who were not ready for the coming of the bridegroom. The 'punchline' is this: 'Keep awake therefore, for you know neither the day nor the hour.' (Matt 25:13)

In the Garden of Gethsemane, he scolded his disciples when they fell asleep: 'Keep awake and pray that you may not come into the time of trial; the spirit indeed is willing, but the flesh is weak.' (Mk 14:38)

In Romans, Paul expands on this very theme:

Besides this, you know what time it is, how it is now the moment for you to wake from sleep. For salvation is nearer to us now than when we became believers; the night is far gone, the day is near. Let us then lay aside the works of darkness and put on the armour of light; let us live honourably as in the day, not in revelling and drunkenness, not in debauchery and licentiousness, not in quarrelling and jealousy. Instead, put on the Lord Jesus Christ, and make no provision for the flesh, to gratify its desires. (Rom 13:11-14)

There's an urgency about the Christian life in between the tick and the tock. The tock is now nearer than the tick. The metaphor of the coming dawn says a lot about the nature of the times. For those who believe, the hopeful light of our salvation is just over the horizon. The coming reign of God is tracing its way into the world, even as we speak.

So, now is not the time for sitting back. The slumbering disciple will miss the opportunity. The old order is passing away – which means dedicating ourselves to the things that belong to the new order of things. Gratifying the hungers of our bodies, and being governed by these drives, is a way of living that smells of death. It is characteristic of the darkness that is being defeated, not the way of the light that is growing. There is, then, an urgency about the Christian life, because we understand ourselves living in a period of amnesty, in which the declaration of the good news of God's forgiveness needs to go out to the world.

This urgency means that for Jesus' disciples there is a dedication to a particular way of life, and a particular mission. That way of life? We know that the day of exposure and judgment is not far. The man who rose from the dead assures us that this is so – that he is coming back, and that there will be no hiding our deeds from him. The Christian is not committed to secret deeds which she thinks are undiscoverable, but acts as if everything about her is done in the bright light of day, in full view.

We also know that the Kingdom of God will be established on earth as it is in heaven. We know, then, that earthly powers – cultural movements, companies, governments, whatever – have their power temporarily and only at God's behest. They may act as if God is absent or non-existent, but they are denying the one from whom they have power in the first place. Their arrogance is ill-founded. The Christian does not fear them, nor does he pursue them. He owes them respect, but no ultimate allegiance whatsoever. The insidious power of social media companies; the nuclear weapons of the superpowers; the economic power of the wealthy; the social pressure exerted in the name of whatever society has decided is right: these powers are not to be feared, for they have no permanence. Before God, they are as nothing. Their power will melt away.

While there is no fear of earthly powers, the Christian is also called to travel light. The things of the world (as we will see) are not bad, but they are not to be trusted. Our possessions, our ambitions, even our families and friends, are to be loved for what they are, and not for what they cannot ever be. They are good, but they do not and cannot secure us in eternity. The protection and the delight they offer us is ephemeral. The Christian life is not a life of no possessions and no pleasures, but it is a life that is not dedicated to possessions or to pleasures. This actually enables us to enjoy the things of the world for what they truly are. We may make decisions to forego possessions or status, since these things are of no ultimate significance.

One of the greatest contemporary terms is FOMO – the 'fear of missing out'. It is an accurate description of the restlessness of soul that grips contemporary Western culture. Can't I have it all? I need to stuff as much as I can into my brief span of time because the curtain is coming down on my life before too long and that will be that. Any missed experience is a tragedy – 'I never got to go to Brazil!' 'I never tried abseiling!' 'I never ate a slice of truffle in a Parisian restaurant!'. But the Christian does not see their life in this way. Because the fullness of eternal life awaits, and because in Christ God grants us all things. As Paul writes in Romans 8:31-32: 'What, then, shall we say in response to these things? If God is for us, who can be against us? He who did not spare his own Son, but gave him up for us all – how will he not also, along with him, graciously give us all things?'

God, we know, is generous beyond all measure. How do we imagine that if we are his we will miss out on anything? There's a kind of peace, a lack of anxiety, made possible by the Christian perspective that enables us to enjoy what we experience with thanksgiving.

2. Where are we?

The New Testament recognises the impending end of all things, and urges Christian disciples not to cling to the things of this world which are passing away. For his part, the apostle Paul opposed 'the flesh' to the 'spirit' – by which he is telling us that, by the Spirit of God, we have an old nature that we need to put to death, and a new, future-wards nature, that we need to cultivate.

But the New Testament authors also recognise the fundamental goodness of the created order. While the world is subject to the powers and principalities of darkness, it retains the basic structure of its good creation. In Romans 1, for example, Paul writes: 'For since the creation of the world God's invisible qualities – his eternal power and divine nature – have been clearly seen, being understood from what has been made, so that people are without excuse.'

That is to say: it is still the case that the creation retains the stamp of its creator. It is still the case that the divine nature radiates through everything he made. If human beings wilfully choose not to see what is there, then that is not because it isn't there. We have no excuse whatsoever for our spiritual blindness.

This means that New Testament Christianity is not what we might called an 'ascetic' faith. An ascetic teaches that the world itself is bad and to be avoided as far as possible. Food and sex in particular are tainted with evil, and we must withdraw from them or be corrupted. Now, there have been Christians who have taught that the life of withdrawal from these things is spiritually superior. But see what Paul says in 1 Timothy 4:1-5:

> The Spirit clearly says that in later times some will abandon the faith and follow deceiving spirits and things taught by demons. Such teachings come through hypocritical liars, whose consciences have been seared as with a hot iron. They forbid people to marry and order them to abstain from certain foods, which God created to be received with thanksgiving by those who believe and who know the truth. For everything God created is good, and nothing is to be rejected if it is received with thanksgiving, because it is consecrated by the word of God and prayer.

'Everything God created is good' says Paul. And he means food and sex in particular. Forbidding marriage and keeping to a selective diet has no intrinsic spiritual value, especially if that comes from the view that somehow these things are bad in and of themselves. That's simply wrong. What you eat and what you drink has no direct spiritual impact on you. Sex within marriage is blessed. These things are not to be forbidden or rejected, but received with thanksgiving to God.

But Christianity is not libertine, either. That is, receiving things with thanksgiving means receiving them as the gifts they were intended by the creator to be. Sexuality is a great and fine gift, and God gives it a particular context for us to enjoy it and find its deeper purpose. Food and drink, likewise, are given to sustain us and give us pleasure. They can become idols and obsessions. We can become gluttons or drunkards. But this is not a problem with the substances themselves.

For this reason, I don't think that a truly biblical stance on drugs and alcohol can ever be an absolute prohibition. These are gifts of the creator. It is up to us to find the right use for these things such that we can unleash their potential for good and restrict their potential for harm. A friend and I used to ask each other, as a kind of theological exercise, 'what might it mean to receive tobacco with thanksgiving?' It's a good question, because it seems that smoking or chewing it is pretty devastating for human health in every regard. Might this be a case of 'thanks but no thanks'? Perhaps. Or maybe we haven't as yet located its best purpose?

Christians, then, enjoy the good gifts of the creator, but do not give themselves over to them. We are not hedonists, but neither are we ascetics. We are aware of the dangers of over-indulgence, and are also aware that our own bodies are gifts from God and need tending. The pleasures of the flesh do not satisfy us spiritually. The hedonist who is also an atheist throws herself at the world because every pleasure has to be wrung out of every last minute. But the Christian knows that there is a greater purpose than pleasure, and a greater pleasure in God than in the world he made.

There's another aspect to this that we need to explore. That's the original commission to Adam and Eve to 'have dominion' over the creation as the creatures made in God's image. Human beings have an ambassadorial role: to represent the creator to his world and to exercise his authority over it in doing what he would have done in it. Of course, this does not give us licence to exploit or damage or destroy. Quite clearly, the creator of heaven and earth is pleased with his work and delights in it. It is precious to him.

Even though we now live in expectation of the radical transformation of the cosmos, we still have a responsibility as human beings for our 'creation mandate'. We cannot now treat the created world as simply something at our disposal or for our use. We are its royal servants, expressing the love of God for his world. Christians, therefore, are truly 'green'. Now, there's some important ways in which a Christian can't agree with a standard 'green' approach. In the first place, human beings are not simply animals with thumbs but have a unique – indeed superior – dignity. There is a value to human life which does not belong to the other creatures. It is not ethical in any situation to farm human beings, for example. We do not treat the euthanasia of elderly cats as akin to the euthanasia of elderly human beings – or at least, we ought not, since they are not comparable cases.

However, the non-human creatures are to be treated with kindness, respect, and empathy. We see this in the Old Testament law, in which animals play a very large part. Israel was an agricultural economy, heavily dependent on animals for protein and other goods. The Sabbath command was given to all creation, not simply human beings – the livestock were also to rest on the seventh day. The command of Deuteronomy 25:4, 'Do not muzzle an ox while it is treading out the grain' recognises that the ox deserves a share of the harvest, since it is working to provide it. It is a living creature, not a machine. In Deuteronomy 22:6, we read: 'If you come across a bird's nest beside the road, either in a tree or on the ground, and the mother is sitting on the young or on the eggs, do not take the mother with the young.'

The purpose of this strange command seems to be to enable animal life to continue. If you take the eggs *and* the mother, then the species cannot survive. The over-fishing of the seas and the hunting of many species to extinction (seen any mammoths lately?) shows the necessity of this law.

Modern industrial farming practices have, in many cases, caused untold suffering and misery to our fellow creatures. Our culture of consumption means that most of us our shielded from the distress of the sow in her tiny stall or the hen in her cage. We have no way of knowing –and little desire to know – whether slaughtering practices are humane. We simply purchase, and eat. And yet, if we see the animals as the precious work of the glorious creator who also made us, and if we understand our own similarity to the animals, and if we remember who we are as human beings, then surely we ought not to stand for this. We need not raise animals to the same dignity as human beings, or find some quality or ability like 'sentience' as a criteria by which we might measure the smarter beasts. This philosophy is usually parallel with a lowering of the dignity and status of the disabled and the unborn. If we simply listen to the Bible, we will be compelled to a better treatment of our fellow creatures without denying the special dignity that we as human beings have.

The same goes for the non-animal creation. The ground, as we learn in Genesis 3, is under a curse, such that our working of it is hard. It still is productive of food and other resources for our comfort and enjoyment, but it comes with complications. In the industrial age, we have become very good at producing food from the ground, and at extracting mineral resources from it. But it seems that a superabundance of food and resources is just as potentially destructive as a lack of them. We can't manage to distribute this massive amount of food evenly across the world, and still some nine million people die of hunger each year – with a reported one in nine people on earth suffering from chronic malnourishment. This seems incredible in the countries where obesity is a significant health problem.

Despite the politics of the matter, there seems no doubt about human-induced climate change, and that we are going to be living in a world changed forever by our addiction to fossil fuels. Even if you disagree with the overwhelming consensus on climate change, it still remains the case that the pollution of the planet we were given by God to manage and rule is a tragedy – a symptom of our rebellion against God and our inability to live up to our calling in the fallen world.

So what are Christians to do? The Christian is not alone, of course, in seeing injustice and harm in the world. However, the Christian has a unique take on the remedy. It is right that we should treat animals with a deeper respect and that we should oppose the exploitative polluting of the planet. We should stand against the sheer wastefulness of our consumer society, with its disposable treatment of created things. These are points to make in the political sphere. But our work as Christians is to preach the gospel in the four corners of the earth as our primary task, since as more people give true regard to the creator of all things, we will find a more selfless humanity. A converted human being who reads the Scriptures will worship the creator of all things, and be attuned to his glory radiating out through his creations. They will receive the good creation with gratitude rather than greed. Just as our best response to poverty is the transformation of lives that the gospel brings, so our best hope for care of the creation is the knowledge of God the creator, who loves the world he made.

3. Who are we?

Who are we then, these creatures who live between the tick and the tock? How we should live is intimately bound up with who we find ourselves to be. In the late 1960s Joni Mitchell warbled:

> We are stardust, we are golden
> We are billion year old carbon
> And we got to get ourselves back to the garden…

It's a beautiful – if confused – blend of random evolution and deliberate creation, science and theology. She was trying to describe the preciousness and fragility of human life, and also a feeling that, somehow, we are not living in the place of original peace anymore.

There's something that meshes here with the biblical view of human being. We are made of the dust, but we have in us the breath of life, the divine energy itself. We are the children of God, 'made a little lower than the angels' and 'crowned with glory and honour', as we read in Psalm 8:

> You have made them a little lower than the angels
> and crowned them with glory and honour.
> You made them rulers over the works of your hands;

you put everything under their feet:
all flocks and herds,
   and the animals of the wild,
the birds in the sky,
   and the fish in the sea,
   all that swim the paths of the seas.

And yet, we are spectacular failures at this mission. We are unworthy of this crown.

In Hebrews 2:5-10, this psalm is taken up by the author and now applied to Jesus Christ. And so we find in him the failure of humanity to be true to its own nature reversed. Jesus completes and fulfils our destiny by being the true human being, always living under God's rule and always serving the world in God's name. He is the true image of the invisible God (Col 1:15, and see Jn 1:14-18).

What becoming a Christian does is recapture and revision our humanity. We are 'born from above' (Jn 3). When we hear the gospel of Jesus Christ, we hear a message which is at first deeply tragic: we have sinned. We are in desperate need of forgiveness. The stench of death and destruction is upon us. When we hear the story of Jesus atoning for our sins – that he has submitted himself to the sentence of death so that we did not have to – and when we believe, it is as if a new person has been created in the old. As Paul says in 2 Corinthians 5:17, 'Therefore, if anyone is in Christ, the new creation has come: The old has gone, the new is here!'

Even though Christians still live in the world that is passing away, and feels the aches and pains and groans of this mortal flesh, they are also people of the future. They belong to the new creation. They are, already, part of the world to come.

The implications of this I don't think we often realise. Paul says 'So from now on we regard no one from a worldly point of view.' (2 Cor 5:16)

We are 'stardust', not by dint of our past, but because of our future. If we are in Christ, we have in us the hope of his resurrection. We have in anticipation the glorious resurrection body which will emerge from the old, like a flower from a seed, or a butterfly from its cocoon. In his great essay 'The Weight of Glory', C.S. Lewis asks us to remember that all human beings are built for an eternal destiny:

> It is a serious thing to live in a society of possible gods and goddesses, to remember that the dullest most uninteresting person you can talk to may one day be a creature which, if you saw it now, you would be strongly tempted to worship, or else a horror and a corruption such as you now meet, if at all, only in a nightmare... There are no ordinary people. You have never talked to a mere mortal. Nations, cultures, arts, civilizations – these are mortal, and their life is to ours as the life of a gnat. But it is immortals whom we joke with, work with, marry, snub, and exploit – immortal horrors or everlasting splendours.

What can it mean to think of ourselves – and others – like this? For starters, I think it changes the way we think about the value of human life and the consequences of our actions. What we do in life (to quote Russell Crowe's *Gladiator*) 'echoes in eternity'. When the gospel of Jesus Christ takes root in a person's heart, this is not merely a choice for them like a preference for a different flavour of ice cream. This is a transformation of their eternal destiny. For Paul, regarding no-one from a worldly point of view means that he is not impressed by worldly attainments or honours. But he is also deeply concerned for the eternal welfare of those he encounters. He poured out his life so that people – even the Gentiles who were by nature his enemies – would know the expectation of the glorious hope of the resurrection of Jesus Christ.

There's nothing abstract about this. In early 2016, I sat by the hospital bed of a woman in my church who was dying of pancreatic cancer. She was a young woman, bright and full of life. Or, she had been. The cancer had robbed her of every ounce of fat, and her skin was a horrid pale grey colour. She drifted in and out of consciousness. It was clear that the end was not far away. Her mother, who was not a church goer, was by her side, and after praying and reading the Bible with my friend, we went to grab a cup of tea. 'Why?' her mother said to me. 'Rebecca believes in God. What does this mean?' I said the only thing I think of at the time: 'this is not the end of the story'.

Rebecca had a faith in Jesus Christ. And that meant that, even as we sat with her decaying body, we were not seeing what she really was, or, I should say, is. The downswing of death was not for her the end; nor did it usher her into something more terrible still. In fact, her death is merely a pause or an interruption in her story. She belongs with the one who was raised gloriously from the dead. And so, we who inhabit this 'vale of tears' grieve not hopelessly or forlornly, but in the expectation of seeing Rebecca once more. These are Paul's words in 1 Thessalonians 4:13-18:

> Brothers and sisters, we do not want you to be uninformed about those who sleep in death, so that you do not grieve like the rest of mankind, who have no hope. For we believe that Jesus died and rose again, and so we believe that God will bring with Jesus those who have fallen asleep in him.

According to the Lord's word, we tell you that we who are still alive, who are left until the coming of the Lord, will certainly not precede those who have fallen asleep. For the Lord himself will come down from heaven, with a loud command, with the voice of the archangel and with the trumpet call of God, and the dead in Christ will rise first. After that, we who are still alive and are left will be caught up together with them in the clouds to meet the Lord in the air. And so we will be with the Lord forever. Therefore encourage one another with these words.

Appendix A:
The Doctrine of Creation and Modern Science

One of the givens of modern life is the supremacy of the scientific world-view. An entity called 'science' has earned its aura in western culture by its many practical achievements in medicine, industry, warfare, engineering and agriculture. Whereas religion deals in the world of the uncertain and intangible, science appeals to hard facts and objectivity. Religious belief is relegated to the realm of the personal; and a wedge is driven between faith and reason.

At the very least, science claims that it renders belief in God unnecessary. In the modern era you can live a healthy and happy life without needing God, because science has provided for us so many benefits. Even worse, the results of scientific study seem in some cases to contradict the claims of Christianity. Science and religion are at war; a war that many people feel only science can win. This is bad news for a doctrine of 'creation', since there cannot be a creation without a creator. What we see around us is not a creation at all, on this account.

Strictly speaking, science is 'knowledge'. But 'science' of course covers a wide range of activities from quantum physics to observing animal behaviours. What these have in common is a method. Science involves finding out things about the natural world by testing ideas against actual data. It rests squarely on the empirical method: its theories are tested by the data we gather with our senses. Scientific theory is thus flexible enough to cope with new data; it acknowledges that it just does its best with the data now available. New data will have to be incorporated by existing theories, and may in fact change them altogether.

But 'science' also refers to a body of knowledge accumulated by the scientific method. Some of this is widely accepted knowledge unlikely to be refuted. But it also includes disputed theories, or speculations. Not all science deals with the certain; rather theories differ in their certainty. It is important to recognise that science is about the collection of facts *and* their interpretation.

It is artificial, however, to see science in abstract, from the people who are called 'scientists'. Science is knowledge which is accepted by a community of scientists: tested nationally and internationally, according to the accepted methods and assumptions of the scientific world. Within this community there are approved and authorised figures. Good science has to meet certain standards, but these standards are set by certain people. This body of people also has a history, with heroes and villains, triumphs and tragedies.

So, to cap it all off, 'science' has become a way of talking in western culture, a discourse. It is something you can appeal to as an authority. You can see this at work in the popular media and in advertising, when you see a man in a white coat with a clipboard in an ad for toothpaste or cosmetics. The aura of science adds an aura of credibility, in the same way that celebrity does. Let me be clear though: science has earned many of its accolades. If I get sick, I am certainly going to be relying on the best that science has to offer.

A state of war, however, is said to exist between the worlds of science and religion and science definitely has the upper hand in the popular mind. The alleged war relates to the history of science and is also fed by some misunderstandings about religion and science as ways of knowing things.

Those who say that science and Christianity are in conflict often point to a series of famous examples in which scientific ideas were opposed by religious groups. These people will also obscure the positive influence of the Christian tradition on the way in which Western science developed. One case that is particularly mentioned is that of Galileo Galilei.

Galileo's case is popularly understood as a battle between a scientific hero and the oppressive Roman Catholic Church. Reality is more complicated, of course. What really occurred was a clash between two types of science – the older Greek science and Galileo's new ideas. Christian theology had been closely linked for many years to the picture of the cosmos outlined by Aristotle and others. This model placed the earth at the centre of the universe rather than the sun. In claiming otherwise, Galileo pitted himself against philosophers and theologians who had a lot to lose. In addition, Galileo came up against an institutional church keen to maintain doctrinal purity in the face of the Reformation.

It is worth noting that Galileo remained a devout Catholic until he died, and never gave up his faith. Further, Galileo was supported and encouraged by some church leaders. It is also worth noting that Galileo's ideas flew in the face of the bulk of scientific opinion at the time, which had very good reasons for its views. The contemporary scientific guild treats outliers in just the same way today – even though they may turn out to be right in the long run.

But on the other side of things, it is true that the claims of science (or what people label 'science') to objectivity and certainty are often wildly exaggerated. 'Science' is held to be a uniquely privileged way of knowing, and purely objective – just as religion is purely subjective.

In the academic world, however, it has long been recognised that the relationship between data and theory in science is far more complex and open-ended than people usually think. As we have seen, science involves collecting data and interpreting it. But there can very often be several plausible interpretations of a set of data. Many factors shape the interpretation of data in science, including creativity, intuition, profit, and ambition. The culture or gender of a scientist may alter or shape his or her findings. Science is not purely objective. Neither is religion purely subjective. It is also an interpretation of a set of data.

It is important for Christians, then, not to isolate theology from science. We need not fear science: if a good God has made an ordered world, though it be distorted by sin, we should expect observation of the natural world not to strike a dissonant chord with his existence. In speaking with non-Christians, who have a great faith in science, it is best not to feel defensive and to feed the conflict theory.

Appendix B: The Millennium

When it comes to thinking about the end of all things, Christians have been heard talking about 'the millennium'. This idea comes from Revelation 20:1-10. It's a dramatic scene:

> And I saw an angel coming down out of heaven, having the key to the Abyss and holding in his hand a great chain. He seized the dragon, that ancient snake, who is the devil, or Satan, and bound him for a thousand years. He threw him into the Abyss, and locked and sealed it over him, to keep him from deceiving the nations any more until the thousand years were ended. After that, he must be set free for a short time. I saw thrones on which were seated those who had been given authority to judge. And I saw the souls of those who had been beheaded because of their testimony about Jesus and because of the word of God. They had not worshipped the beast or its image and had not received its mark on their foreheads or their hands. They came to life and reigned with Christ for a thousand years. (The rest of the dead did not come to life until the thousand years were ended.) This is the first resurrection. Blessed and holy are those who share in the first resurrection. The second death has no power over them, but they will be priests of God and of Christ and will reign with him for a thousand years. When the thousand years are over, Satan will be released from his prison and will go out to deceive the nations in the four corners of the earth – Gog and Magog – and to gather them for battle. In number they are like the sand

on the seashore. They marched across the breadth of the earth and surrounded the camp of God's people, the city he loves. But fire came down from heaven and devoured them. And the devil, who deceived them, was thrown into the lake of burning sulphur, where the beast and the false prophet had been thrown. They will be tormented day and night for ever and ever

Now, to what exactly does this refer? How much does the Book of Revelation chart out a map of history? There are basically three main explanations of the millennium.

For some Christians, the 1,000 years occurs within history, and will lead up to the return of Jesus Christ. As that period of time progresses, the gospel of Jesus Christ will also advance throughout the world. For many in this camp, the millennium has already begun. This is the position called *post-millennialism.*

Others, holding a position called *pre-millennialism,* say that the millennium is an extension of history after Christ's return – a kind of 'extra-time', to use a footballing metaphor. The 'pre' in 'pre-millennialism' is there because Christ's return precedes the 1,000 years. During the 1,000 years, the gospel will gradually triumph on the earth. Pre-millennialist views – of which there are a wide variety – often have a particular role for the modern state of Israel, and talk about 'the rapture', when a particular group of Christians will be taken to heaven.

A third group would say that the millennium in fact describes the whole of history as it has panned out between the first and second coming of Christ. Like many of the numbers in Revelation, the 1,000 is symbolic rather than literal. The preaching of the gospel because of the missionary activity of the apostles and their descendants binds Satan. This view (probably the majority view) is called *amillennialism.*

Although this is an issue on which I think there can be tolerance of different views, I am firmly of the view that this third option best suits the biblical evidence. It best fits with how the book of Revelation asks us to read it. The other views also invite us to speculate in a very unhelpful way about whether the return of Christ has come – in just such a way as Jesus himself seems to forbid with his warnings about knowing not the day nor the hour. New Testament Christians aren't those who look for portents as to the meaning of the events around them and what is about to take place. They have the key information, which is that Jesus Christ has risen from the dead, and will one day return to judge the world. That tells us enough about the times in which we are living.

Appendix C: The Spiritual Creation

In the Apostle's Creed, Christians testify that God the Father is not simply the maker of the earth, but also of another realm, namely 'heaven'. What can we say about this other sphere? We are immediately struck by the problem of interpreting the Bible aright in this area. There is no doubt that the Bible testifies to a heaven, repeatedly and strongly.

Yet in doing so, it deploys cosmological language and concepts that we have to adapt to some degree. The first references in the Bible clearly refer to the realm above the earth – the materially solid dome on which the lights were fixed and which held back the waters in the sky. But this was already vested with a theological significance; for Israel was clear that heaven was where the Lord dwelt in his glory, as opposed to the fertility gods/goddesses, who were definitely of the earth, or the monstrous deities of the sea. Heaven subsequently became a shorthand for the place in which and from which the God of Israel rule and judged. The heavenly throne was the royal judgement seat (Ps 2:4; Is 66:1). Israel's tabernacle and her temple were (as the Letter to the Hebrews clarifies) earthly analogies of the heavenly throne room and served as illustrations of the kind of business that is conducted in heaven – justice, and atonement.

But we have to note the element of mystery and reserve here. As the Swiss theologian Karl Barth writes: 'Reserve is demanded because, although heaven as the place of God is known as a place, as another created place, as a higher cosmic sphere confronting our own, beyond these delimiting definitions it is unknown and inconceivable, and therefore a mystery.'

Heaven is by definition a realm inaccessible to eyes smeared with sin. We must speak very carefully, and not fall prey to the temptation to elaborate a kind of map of heaven – as if we could. The ascension of Jesus is the doctrine that helps us most here. His resurrection body fits him, as the 'man from heaven' (1 Cor 15) for his reign in heaven. His ascension is to a throne of judgement and authority. In Acts 1, Jesus ascends, with all the royal and priestly significance this implies. The angel who remains says to the disciples 'why do you stand here looking into the sky? This same Jesus who has been taken from you into heaven, will come back in the same way you have seen him go into heaven.'

In some sense we are to understand heaven as superior to the earth, a higher realm, in which the reign of God in Christ is complete ahead of his victory on earth. In Psalm 8, we hear that we are made a little 'lower' than the angels. Is this anything but a spatial idea? There is, we are reminded in Scripture, a gap between how things are in heaven and how things are on earth. We pray that God's kingdom would come on earth as it is in heaven (using Matthew's notion of the kingdom of 'heaven') – things are not yet on earth what they are in heaven's kingdom. There still remains the complete revelation and finalisation of God's rule on the earth.

What of the creatures that populate this other sphere? We are used to trivialising angels. They feature so often in the most sentimental forms of popular culture that we are inclined not to take them very seriously, or not to know what to do with them. Yet, Scripture testifies to their existence, without at the same time giving us a complete angelology. Though the word *angelos* can of course simply mean 'messenger' (which could mean a human being fulfilling the role), it is quite clear that what is most often meant by the term is some kind of heavenly being.

It is worth following the hunch of starting with the involvement of angels in the identification of Jesus Christ as the Son of God. At the key events in the life of the Saviour, angels stand as markers of the boundary between the heavens and the earth. Gabriel, one of the few named angels, appears to Mary (Lk 2). The birth of Jesus is attended by the massed choirs of heaven. Jesus is tended by angels during his time in the wilderness. There are angels at the empty tomb; there is the angel in Acts 1 at the Ascension of Jesus. At each point, the angels are a signpost pointing to the divine work in Christ. They bracket the virgin's womb and the empty tomb as the places in which an ordinary human explanation will not do.

These are salvation-historical moments. Once again, we should note the Bible's lack of a theory of angels. It keeps them concealed from our view. We cannot pin them to a board and study them like butterflies. Worship of angels is a terrible mistake (as Hebrews seems to indicate). Likewise, the obsession with creating hierarchies and schemas of angel is dangerous distraction. In the sixth century, the mystic Pseudo-Dionysius[1] offered an elaborate description of the angelic hierarchies in his books *The Celestial Hierarchy* and *The Ecclesiastical Hierarchy*.

---

1 He's called 'Pseudo-Dionysius' not because his mother called him that, but because he purports to be Dionysius the Areopagite, who Paul meets in Acts 17. He obviously cannot be that man, but we don't know his real name.

Pseudo-Dionysius required angels to complete his vision of an entirely hierarchical cosmos, with God as the high point from which all things emanated and to which all things would return. The celestial hierarchy was formed by three classes of angel: the cherubim and the seraphim; the dominions; and the powers, principalities and authorities. This hierarchy matched the ecclesiastical hierarchy of bishops, priests, deacons and laity. Pseudo-Dionysius' description gained wide acceptance in the Western church. Eventually, angels were seen to carry out the entire of God's providential action.

Scripture does indeed teach the ranking of angelic beings. But the Reformers of the 16th Century denied the specific details of the Dionysian system. So what can we affirm? That like us, angels are numerous, created, spiritual, rational and moral. But Scripture affirms that only humans are made in the image of God (see Psalm 8; Heb 2). As Augustine puts it: 'God gave to no other creature than man the privilege of being after his own image'. The angel is a spiritual, and not an enfleshed being. Angels therefore do not have the common bond of a species formed through bodily reproduction. Angels witness God's salvation, but are not its objects – they are its servants.

What about the enemies of the angels – the demons? We should be aware that demons, even more than angels, lie at the periphery of Scripture's account of the world. We catch a glimpse of them only out of the corner of one eye. Once again, it is the story of Jesus Christ that brings out the demonic and the satanic in force. The appearance of the demons is as much a sign of his identity as the appearance of angels – a kind of negative counterpart to it. The demon who says 'what do you want of us, Son of the Most High?' in Mark 1 has a kind of perverse insight into Jesus that the disciples are slow to share. The key parable is the story of the strong man in Mark 3:20-30. In this teaching, Jesus proclaims the prior 'tying up' of Satan – that's his defence against the accusation that he has an evil spirit.

Where do the demons and the devil come from? The theological tradition has proposed that they are fallen angels, on the basis of passages like Isaiah 14:12 where the king of Babylon is described as the radiant star (Lucifer) cast down from heaven. Jude 6 is the clearest verse that seems to describe an angelic fall of some nature. There are also sinning angels in 2 Peter 2:4. Karl Barth, however, warns against us making too much of these texts: it was one of the 'bad dreams of the older dogmatics', as he puts it. His solution was to say that these beings have their origin in non-being – in 'nothingness'. Everything they are is a 'not'; they are 'being which exists only as it denies all true being'. They exist because God judges and repudiates all that is counter to his will. The advantage of this reading of the matter is that no independent power is given to these agents of chaos. They are merely parasitic.

That there is a place where God's rule is unopposed, where his will is done, gives us hope as we pray for his will to be done on the earth. What we are praying for is only for him to finish what he has established. There is no essential dualism here, no war in the heavens to mirror the war on earth. Satan's defeat is assured. There are therefore no grounds for excessive interest in demonic beings, or in exorcisms. The gospel itself is a triumphant exorcism of all that stands opposed to the holy God. Likewise, the angels point us away from interest in themselves and towards the reality of God's kingdom established on heaven.